Lake Letters

VOLUME ONE

Lake Letters

Letters to Lake Michigan

Poetry &
Essay collection

Mae Stier

ISBN 978-0-578-59979-3

All photographs were taken by Mae Stier.

Many of these pieces appeared in various forms in a number of publications. I would like to thank the editors of each who shared my words and my love of Lake Michigan:
The Boardman Review, The Glen Arbor Sun, Northerly Magazine, Looking Deeply, Driftless, and Lake Effect Co.
Publication design by Isaac Daniels.

To the lake, *always*

Spring

Summer

Autumn

Winter

I Measure Time

I measure time
by how the Lake moves,
her body of water ever-changing.
Calm and quiet at dawn,
boisterous by mid-day.
Evening falls, the blue air darkens,
purple waves crash into night.

Again it is morning
and chaos rages on, surf
rattles the stones on the shore
and I forget about time,
lose my measure
of what is not this water.
I am undone watching her sway,

entire days drowned
in her depths.

Spring

Barefoot Days

B arefoot days. We have waited all winter for them, for the chance to slip out of our shoes and dip our toes into a still-cold Lake Michigan. You sense them approaching on the wind, each morning slightly warmer than the last, but it is the light that truly ushers the season in. The way the orange fades to red at sunset, the way the sun creeps its way further north every day. Light slants through the window to wake you in the morning and however quietly, announces the arrival of Spring.

The light changes first and then the landscape—brown and barren suddenly bursting bright green. Wild onions and trillium carpet the woods and soon the maples explode neon. Next comes the forsythia, yellow and wild through the streets of town, calling forth the arrival of the lilacs. They are the true crown of a country spring, the air fragrant with their scent. All of northern Michigan is drenched in it.

It is in the early months of spring where our daily patterns change. We trade our boots for sandals far earlier than we really ought and step outside every chance we get. The first warm day when the thermometer reaches fifty feels like a miracle, feels to us in April as eighty degrees will feel in August. We trade hats and winter coats for bare arms and excitement.

On these early spring days the answer is always yes to the invitation to go outside. Winter was filled with excuses—the roads were too icy or I just needed a night in—but spring is the casting off of responsibility. There is nothing more important than being in the sun, nothing you need more than running down the sand dunes to stand on the shore of Lake Michigan.

So we take to the dunes every chance we get. The dunes themselves call to us, shining like beacons in the glow of the sun as it returns from its winter hiding. Staying out later, showing itself from behind the haze of clouds where it spent the last few months, the sun lights up the hills like a neon marquee. It announces *Tonight Only: Warm Sand on Your Toes*, and we act accordingly. We forget that spring turns to summer and we have months before we must return to icy winter. We roll down the dunes as if it is our last chance to do so.

Moving through the seasons in northern Michigan causes us to pay attention. To prepare. To change our patterns. The length of the days changes, the scenery goes from brown to neon to dark green to white, and we track our lifetime within the colors. For now, spring has arrived and we track mud from ground that was recently frozen into our houses and our cars. All of it is a reminder that time is passing. All of it is an opportunity to pause and smell the earth, to listen to the rain as it glides through the gutters, to try and catch sight of the first bud as it emerges from the trees.

We move into this new season with renewed energy. Winter had its own place in the cycle of the year, created space for us to rest and to plan. We needed it. But the arrival of the wild plants in the woods and the sun lingering later over the dunes is another necessity entirely. It is one we welcome all the more fervently for the many dark nights we spent waiting for it.

The arrival of spring invites us into a world of color and sound, of carelessness and adventure. It invites us to first swims in water that is barely above forty, to bonfires on the beach welcoming in later nights. It invites us to climb the dunes so that we may take in the sun, take in the view, and then dares us—with all the reclaimed recklessness of warmer days—to run down as fast as we can without falling.

"Moving through the seasons in northern Michigan causes us to pay attention."

A Spring Wind

Waves roll in the haze
of summer air kissing
winter water,
a spring wind
that settles onshore
to coax bare trees
into bursting forth.
"It's time," the waves call,
the trees at attention,
pulsing
with invisible life.

Resurrection

Notice the rebirth
of daffodils in early May,
ferns unfurling in flower beds
as we sit inside and ponder
what lies beyond death.
Forsythia returns to life
out the window, the Lake
thaws and invites us
again to be baptized.
We worry over mortality,
meanwhile the earth
practices endless
resurrection.

Steady Waves

When I am unsure of my voice
I go to the Lake, to practice
speaking what I have learned
to keep quiet.

I mutter as I walk the shore,
my voice in a crescendo,
drowning fearful words
in the cadence

of steady waves.

Takeover

Lake levels rise
as waves crawl further
up the beach.
The water, more powerful
than our attempts
to stop it, takes over sand
and dune grass. All we can do
is watch.

Treasures

I go to the edge of the Lake,
bright and quiet in the morning.
Sand littered in Petoskey stones,
jasper, rose quartz.

Flea market
of natural treasures,
a history lesson
predating any book.

The weight of the earth
compressed into stone,
shining in the white light
of the sun.

A Lesson From My Lake Obsession

I reserve an awe
for you that I withhold
from myself, amazement
for the wild ways you change
without warning. Unpredictable
shifts from one day to the next.

I marvel at your inconsistency
while criticizing my own.
If only I held the same regard
for myself as I do for you, my waves
allowed to rage with no attempt
to restrain them.

Nature Cues

The morning unfolds in a haze.
Dunes blanketed in fog,
water calm and icy grey.

Silence.

Only the call of the seagulls,
the dull tap of the Lake
touching sand, then receding.

I take my cue
and watch.

Begin Anew

I have felt waves
rolling in my bones,
days of chaos despite the calm
of you. Smooth glass reflecting blue skies—
the opposite of my haze.

Soon you will kick up wild,
trade your silence for turbulence
by a shift of the wind
or dip in temperature. A small change
in energy could transform me, too.

The days begin anew
and everything can change.

First Swim

I scream
as I run in,
under.

Splash,
silence.

Your quiet
drowns out
my noise.

Summer

Secret Beach

T his stretch of shoreline is empty despite the early summer warmth, and I throw down my towel and pull a book from my backpack. The perfect afternoon—a break from the busyness of the village where tourists hurry in and out of the shops and restaurants. A quiet place to rest in the sun. I can see families a half mile north at a popular beach, splashing in the shallows of Lake Michigan's still-cool water, but their laughter doesn't carry to where I lay on my secret beach. I open my book to the first page, hardly making it to the next before the laziness of the summer afternoon overtakes me. I drift asleep to the sound of the waves and of seagulls calling each other overhead.

This is my favorite getaway: a secret beach that feels like an extension of my own backyard, an oasis I escape to every chance I get. I could tell you where it is (I won't), but that probably isn't necessary, as you have likely already filled in the image with scenes of your own. An abandoned road through the woods or an old trail lined with dying ash trees or brilliant birch. There are dozens of tucked away beaches in northern Michigan and magically, when you talk about yours I have no idea where it is.

This region has become a tourist destination, with a national park that invites visitors to explore the great outdoors. Each year, more visitors come to the area and each year the quiet stretches of shoreline diminish in number. The beaches that were once unknown have now been revealed by the local tourism magazines. Each summer we become more secretive of our beach haunts, resolve to tell fewer people about them. We cannot lose yet another hideaway to a vacationer.

Truth be told, I found my secret beach before most would say I had earned it. I was visiting with friends who had never been to the area, and we were looking for a place to sleep under the stars and next to the Lake. I diligently searched for options until I found this beach and I drove them down an old dirt road not knowing what to expect. We showed up just in time to watch the sun set over the water and I fell in love with the way the pine and birch trees pushed right up against the dunes. Years later when I finally moved here, I wandered down that old dirt road to see if I could

45

"I know these secret slivers of quiet water abound if you take the time to find them."

still access the same shoreline. I could and miraculously it was as quiet as the first time I had encountered it.

The road has been shut down for a few years now, which makes it even harder to access. I am grateful for this. In the summer, I bike down the bumpy trail, dodging fallen trees that cross my path. No one makes an attempt to clear them now that the road is closed. At the end of the trail, I lean my bike against one of the old maples—no need to lock it when no one is around—and run down the dune to bask in the sun. Even in the winter, I make my way to this deserted trail, ski down the old road to the edge of the dune and slide down in my boots.

In some ways it feels like this spot belongs to me, though of course the land is public and I have no right to call it mine. There is something that feels empowering about having a few hundred yards of beach to yourself in vacationland, but I know these secret slivers of quiet water abound if you take the time to find them. I did nothing to deserve this beach of mine that isn't mine at all, and I have no ownership over it. I simply took the time to look beyond what was marked on the map and let an old dirt road be the guide.

Light

Sunlight pours
through translucent waves,
blue-green glow
just before

the break.

Shadows of splashing
dance on the beach,
and I leap
to avoid getting wet.

Ripples in the sand
as the water recedes,
washed away
by the next wave.

Everything visible and then—
gone.
Shadow and then—
light.

Light, Again

The sun
makes waves
on my skin
through the smooth
surface of the Lake,
reminds me
I can still find
the light.

Summer's Symphony

A storm moves over the Lake,
grey-blue clouds pushing
eastward to shore, the dunes
bright in contrast. Thunder
warns of what is coming
as lightning electrifies the horizon.
Summer's symphony,
the crack
in the distance. Rain
batters
the water.
The movement
of hot air over a cool Lake
exploding into anthem.

The first warm swim

feels like relief,
like coming home
to bread in the oven.

The scent alone
fills you.

Sunday Morning

Sunday morning
I put on my best for you,
walk to your edge
and open my heart to you,
jump in to feel
your cool embrace.

I suck holy water
from my shoulders, your
freshness mixed
with my sweat,
divine body
cleansing flesh.

Summer

My bed
is full of sand
and my sheets
smell
like Lake water.

For February

When deep in the slow days
of summer, remember
to store some sunshine
for February.

To the Lake, in the Midst of Busy Summer

You are a moment of calm,
the second-hand stopped
with no one to notice,
an early Sunday morning
with no place to be.

You are a cool breeze
after a summer storm, the relief
that cracks the heat.
Raindrops making puddles
in the street.

You are a breath,
ribs expanding before the exhale,

a pause

that slows everything down.

Swimming Lessons

I pictured my life a quiet river:
fluid movement in one direction,
carving deeper into the banks
of a predestined path.

I would float down the middle of it,
leisurely for the most part, carried
by the current to a destination
that made sense of the winding.

Instead life seems to be a Lake:
a pool of moments both wild and tranquil,
crashing into each other and changing direction
based on the wind.

The water around me moves only
to itself and I work to choose a direction
in the midst, each new wave teaching me
new ways to swim.

Home

I have been
weightless
in your waves
when I needed
carrying
most.

Autumn

Lake/Home

It begins with the Lake. It always does for me. The story of how I found myself in a small northern Michigan town on the brink of my thirties, living alone in a tiny house and writing poetry every chance I get, only makes sense if I mention Lake Michigan.

It begins before I can really remember, sometime before I was five when the memories are still hazy and exist mostly as colors and objects: the green leather couch in my Grandparents' family room, the worn wooden steps that led from their house down to the beach. My recollection of it all, a warm orange. Faint memories that are mostly feelings—a cool stone placed in my hand, crashing waves that knock me over—embedded in my body. I return to them now as distant dreams.

The memory-feelings stayed tucked away for awhile as I tried on different places to call home, different relationships, different jobs. I bounced between cities, between coasts, in and out like the waves. Always I would return to northern Michigan—for a long weekend of camping, for a family vacation, for a friend's wedding—but for years I let myself walk out of this place, intent on finding somewhere else to call my own.

I tried northern California for a time, and while living in a cold apartment in the city I would lay on the couch and listen to music that reminded me of Lake Michigan. It made me cry with a desire that surprised me. Through the light and noise of the city moving outside my window, I dreamt of the quiet air of the lakeshore, the breeze moving through the maples on a summer night, the feeling of walking on the sand after midnight with nothing but the moon to light my way. As the soundtrack to my dreams, I heard Lake Michigan touching the sand, sometimes wildly with the crash of mighty waves and sometimes with the soft touch of a mother on her sleeping child. The hazy beach fires of my youth warmed my sleep with their memory.

Eventually, the warmth of those dreams begged me home, begged me to the shoreline I always tried to visit but had never imagined living on. It was vacationland and living in the community full time seemed largely reserved for retirees. I couldn't picture a life there in my late twenties. I was afraid I would get too lonely or that I wouldn't be able to do the type of

work I wanted to do without the hustle of city life. Still, my body knew its home and I moved anyway.

Returning to this lakeshore awakened something in me, required me to pay more attention than I was prone to doing elsewhere. What is it about nature that has a tendency to do that? I walked barefoot in the sand and would feel the way it pressed up between my toes. I smelled the opening lilacs in the spring and suddenly noticed the whole world opening. I was opening, too. To myself. To the life I really wanted. I started writing every day, mostly to Lake Michigan and mostly as an expression of the sense of home I had found. I had searched all over the country to find it, had spent years trying to create it in relationships, and here it was the same stretch of shoreline where I visited during my childhood summers: home.

I experienced the seasons in new ways in my new home, celebrated the arrival of September as only those in vacation towns do when our hiking trails and beaches quiet down and we find the time again to enjoy them. Autumn leaves turned brighter than I had ever seen them, maybe because it was northern Michigan or maybe because life had slowed enough that I could finally notice it. I drove down seasonal roads in a car that could barely manage the terrain just to see the color, stopping in the middle of the dirt roads to take photos of the leaves.

I am just thirty miles from where my Grandparents lived when I was young, from where we sat on the beach and looked for stones and made s'mores around a fire that was licked by the shallow waters of the Lake. There are new memories being made in a smaller house a few more steps from the beach that look different than my younger memories. The breadth of what I have experienced between my first Lake Michigan encounters until now has changed the way that I interact with this magic place. But even with all of the travel and heartache and life that has been lived, Lake Michigan still calls me as always. The Lake still begs me in to experience the crashing waves, to pick up stones from along the edge. To find myself on this shoreline that is changing and unchanged all at once, in much the same way I am.

Summer's Aftertaste

The trees were covered
in autumn confetti,
the air still warm.
Summer's aftertaste.
I stood on the shore
next to the blue bath
of you and felt my size,
miniscule compared
to your expanse.

My heart clenched
over phone calls
not received, summer
attention fading like the leaves
on the trees. I cried
to you, stripped
to my underwear and waded in,
married lonely tears
to your soothing water.

Searching

I have asked hundreds
of questions of your waves,
cried to the depths for answers
and only found one or two.

But I have loved the days
spent searching, digging up stones
and learning to hold my breath
underwater.

Secret

You have been still
for days, no wave
sneaking in to crease
your surface. Quiet,
like you hold a secret.

I have been wind
and waves, the tumult
as a storm rolls in,
announcing myself
with darkness and thunder.

I sit in the sand to dull
my edges, to be close
and listen to your silence.
To learn your secret
and keep it.

Awe

The color feels impossible,
a palette you couldn't imagine.

How is that smoky grey
kissing crystal clear teal?

Unravel

I unravel
like the hem
of my too-worn jeans,
the rug in front of my kitchen
sink. The waves rolling
down shore, becoming separate
from one another.

Wildness

I watch waves crash
on the sand, pulling rocks
into a world of movement.
Stones roll across each other

making music like a rainstick.
The slow rhythm of turning,
a beat with an uncontrolled fury.
The stones moved this way

for years until this morning,
when on a quiet walk
I bend down to hold one
in my hand,

roll it gently over my palm,
marveling
that such soft edges
could be born from wildness.

Tideless Lake

You move as though the moon
pulls you, but its sway is nominal
when compared to the wind,
the atmospheric pressure,
the will of your waves
to creep up the shore
and caress the dunes,

reminding me I do not need
a moon to move.

The Roar

The symphony of worry
in my mind

>   *—all the fear*
> *I have created, the lists*
> *I have made, the things*
> *I thought I needed—*

falls silent in the roar
of your waves.

Winter

Winter's Imposition

I moved to northern Michigan in January, in the midst of a mild Michigan winter. My neighbors reminded me of its benign temperatures all year, warning that a real winter would take me by surprise. As I stood at the beach in August next to village locals I had only just met, they warned me "just wait until winter really hits."

So I waited. I waited without much forethought, immersed in the perfection of summer on Lake Michigan, enamored with the rhythms of this tiny village. I walked to the Lake daily, bumping into my neighbors along the way as they walked their dogs or headed home from the post office in shorts and t-shirts. At the beach I watched as tourists circled in their minivans to find an open parking spot, watched the yellow-vested parking attendant diligently ensure those without a village parking pass had paid the fee. On Friday nights the locals took over the last lot, perched themselves on the wall between the sidewalk and the beach with wine and cheese to share. Everyone would stay well past the 9:30 sunset, lighting fires and lingering late into the night.

As the water warmed up and the season droned on, I spent entire afternoons swimming in Lake Michigan, kayaking and paddle boarding the nearby rivers and lakes. When Lake Michigan was calm, I would paddle on her, too. I rode my bicycle on the scenic drive before sunset some nights, passing carloads of tourists at each lookout, the Lake Michigan overlook atop the dune covered in hundreds of bodies. Most nights I ate dinner in my backyard to the sound of birds chirping overhead, the rustling of leaves as the deer would catch sight of me and turn to run back into the bushes. If I woke up early enough I could catch them grazing in my yard at dawn, feasting before the rest of the village began to stir.

November brought faint dustings of snow to cover leftover autumn leaves and abandoned summer houses, flurries that were followed by forty degree days and a melt. Maybe this winter would again be mild. But by December my little house was buried in snow, each day dumping more than the day before, hemming me in. I started each day in the driveway, digging a way out. Life began to slow down, trickling out ever so slightly like the water from my

117

pipes; the shower constantly dripping to ward off a freeze.
Lake Michigan grew colder each day, the snow forming further
and further offshore so that now in January, it is falling on us
almost constantly.

It is safe to say that winter has arrived. A real winter, the kind
that makes me nostalgic for childhood and snow forts and ice
skating on frozen lakes. The kind of winter my neighbors have
been warning me about all year—roads left unplowed for days,
temperatures hovering close to zero, lake effect snow my landlord
shovels off the roof.

All year I expected to not be overly surprised by the winter they
warned me of. But as I sit in what feels very much like a snow
globe, I cannot help but be astonished. Winter demands my
attention, and I wonder now if this is what my neighbors were
preparing me for. Perhaps they were not telling me what I could
not handle, but they were waiting to see if I would appreciate the
engagement winter requires. The way winter imposes itself upon
me, requiring that I savor it with intention.

I still see all the same neighbors outside everyday, dressed
now in parkas and thick winter caps as they walk their dogs and
trudge to the post office. I still run into friends at the beach for
sunset. Now, instead of sprawling on blankets around campfires or
perching atop the wall, we huddle in our cars sipping hot tea out
of thermoses, hoping the sun will peek out from behind the winter
clouds. The fire rings have been pulled off the beach, the trash cans
and picnic tables tucked away. A little more ice forms
on the shoreline each day. The scenic drive is closed until spring,
and the only way to access the best views of Lake Michigan is to
cross country ski or snowshoe to the lookouts. We don our gear
and do this often.

The land looks foreign all covered in white, the deer are more
plump and they come closer to my house in search of whatever
food they can find. Last night I walked the shoreline and watched
from afar as a deer stood on its hind legs, eating the leaves off
a cedar tree. When I came home and settled into bed, I could hear
a deer doing the same just outside my window and then huddling

against my house for warmth. Rabbits have created a home under my front porch.

It is true that my encounters with Lake Michigan are less immersive in this frozen season. I stay tucked away more than I do in the summer. The village streets are quiet most days and I walk right down the middle of them to avoid the snow-covered sidewalks. The parking lot at the beach is empty and unplowed. Even still, I walk the shoreline. I layer my body in fleece-lined pants, pull on a pair of hefty boots, stuff hand-warmers into my gloves and walk down to watch as ice slowly takes over the surface of the Lake, snow quietly falling from the sky.

"Winter imposes itself upon me, requiring that I savor it with intention."

January Sun

It is deceiving
to see sun on the Lake
in January.

The shudder of light
bouncing on water,
seeming to call us in.

Meanwhile, frozen noses
while standing onshore
in ten degree air.

We turn from the invitation,
the Lake left to freeze—
alone, quiet.

Lessons in Showing Up

Your waves roll
different each day,
but your presence
is constant.
Regardless of season
or wind on the shore
you are here.
I am invited
to be as well.

Slow Progress

I walked to the Lake last night,
found ice where open water
had just been. It felt so sudden,
like the change from day to night,
evolution unseen,
made visible.

Ignoring what was not obvious,
for months I forgot the Lake
could freeze, forgot it was changing
each day as my nose
turned red in the wind
and I watched the waves
roll in as always.

Had I only reached out
a hand to touch the water,
I would have felt
the shift,
slow progress.

Warm to cool
to cold
to ice.

Open water frozen over
in an instant.
The Lake would disagree.

Winter:

a season in greyscale,
snow and sky blending
in a dull marriage,
a colorless world,
saved only by the blue
of Lake Michigan—
a taste of summer's light
in February.

Blue

Engulfed
by viridian, I sink
into a state of blue. Air
restricted, lungs constricting,
teal waves closing around me. I become
a stone, a rock of hard pressed minerals, born
in another age when the waters were ice and the land
was hidden below. Ageless and at once ancient,
a piece of history pulled under the depths
to roll on the floor of this glacial Lake,
to be discovered in another ten
thousand years, in another
age, edges softened
by centuries

of waves,

of sand,

of blue.

Midwinter

The sun stands still
and the world holds its breath,
anticipating longer days.

Snow dusts the shoreline
and gleams like diamonds,
just before the light dips

below the Lake. Waves churn
in the longest night, a song to remind
us time still moves forward.

Morning is coming and with it—
light. Day will soon again
overtake the night.

Wednesday Morning

Everything is frozen
and I slide to the edge
of the rocks, look down
at the Lake. Droplets
of ice careen at my cheeks,
and I return to the car
red and chapped.

A brisk hello,
a wake-up moment,
whatever you call it I
feel it
an hour later, my skin still raw
from the frozen air,
my heart still pounding
from exhilaration.

Softness

The softness
of the winter shoreline,
blankets of snow
settled on mounds of ice.
The silence of a nursery
as the baby sleeps, broken
by a gust of wind
wrapping its arms
around everything.

About the author

Mae Stier is a writer and photographer living in northern Michigan. She graduated from Grand Valley State University with a BFA in Creative Writing. She writes poetry and creative non-fiction, and in 2018 began a project called "Letters to Lake Michigan" inspired by her love of the Great Lake. The project began by mailing a poem a day to individuals who subscribed to the project online, and poem subscriptions are still available through her website letterstolakemichigan.com. Since the initial project began, her poetry and essays have been featured in a number of local publications in the Midwest. She lives with her partner, their dog, and newborn son in Empire, Michigan.

Acknowledgements

This project would not have been possible without the support of so many. To all of the strangers and friends who signed up for the initial "Letters to Lake Michigan" poetry subscription, thank you for your love of the water and your encouragement of my writing practice. It is through that project that I was able to create a system for self-publishing, if even in small ways. Thank you to Interlochen Academy of Arts and Holly Wren Spauling for offering programs for adults to continue to hone their crafts and for the inspiration to mail little poems into the world. Thank you to the publications who have shared my writing including: The Boardman Review, The Glen Arbor Sun, Driftless, Looking Deeply, Northerly Mag, Lake Effect Co., City Chapel and The Fresh Exchange.

To those who helped turn a year's worth of poetry into a collection, I am grateful for your time and the energy you put forward. To my dear friend Lindsey Bandy and my brother Garrett Stier, thank you for reading through all of the pieces I sent your way and for helping to narrow down the collection into one cohesive unit. You have both been constant encouragers of my work even before this project came into existence and I know that I would not be as dedicated to this craft if it were not for you both creating the space for me to share my words with you along the way. Thank you to Ted Velie and Sam Brown for your assistance in editing as the publication came together and to Spencer McQueen and Bryan Laubhan for their artful critique of the photos and design of the publication. Thank you to Isaac Daniels for designing such a beautiful book to showcase my words better than I could have pictured.

Lake Michigan, you deserve your own thank you as you are the inspiration for this project and for so much of my life. Thank you for being constant even as you change and for teaching me so much about caring for the world around us. Living near you has made me better.

I am grateful to my parents, Ron and Diane Stier, for always encouraging me to create, and to my mom especially for the books she read us as children and into adulthood that cultivated my love of words. Thank you for making us write poems on family vacation.

To my incredibly supportive and sweet partner, Tim Egeler. Thank you for being understanding of the long hours I dedicated to this project during such a busy time in our lives and for always listening to the early drafts of my words. Thank you for believing in me and for making me feel like my words matter. I could not imagine a better human to assist me with creating this project and with creating the tiny human who will soon join us out here in the world. Thank you does not even begin to cover it.

And lastly, thank YOU: the one holding this publication in your hands. Whether you were drawn by your own love of Lake Michigan or because you read a poem that resonated, I am grateful for your support.